About the Author

Growing up in rural Kentucky, Jim Duff never imagined himself as being an author of a book. His passion for reading came to him after he graduated school in 1990. Jim is a father, poet, writer, songwriter, musician, music producer and cancer survivor.

Pantheon of the Senses

Jim Duff

Pantheon of the Senses

Olympia Publishers
London

www.olympiapublishers.com
OLYMPIA PAPERBACK EDITION

Copyright © Jim Duff 2023

The right of Jim Duff to be identified as author of
this work has been asserted in accordance with sections 77 and 78
of the Copyright, Designs and Patents Act 1988.

All Rights Reserved

No reproduction, copy or transmission of this publication
may be made without written permission.
No paragraph of this publication may be reproduced,
copied or transmitted save with the written permission of the
publisher, or in accordance with the provisions
of the Copyright Act 1956 (as amended).

Any person who commits any unauthorised act in relation to
this publication may be liable to criminal
prosecution and civil claims for damage.

A CIP catalogue record for this title is
available from the British Library.

ISBN: 978-1-80439-214-0

This is a work of fiction.
Names, characters, places and incidents originate from the writer's
imagination. Any resemblance to actual persons, living or dead, is
purely coincidental.

First Published in 2023

Olympia Publishers
Tallis House
2 Tallis Street
London
EC4Y 0AB

Printed in Great Britain

Dedication

I dedicate this book to the loving memory of Robert Hicks.

Acknowledgements

Thank you to Robert Hicks for always believing in me. Thank you to Kristina for speeding up time. Thank you to Olympia Publishing for turning a dream into a reality.

Characters:

1. Reighlon (the God of Love. Dwells in the North.)

2. Shaylah (is the female emanation of Reighlon.)

The language they speak is "ba Kay sha kosh".

3. Luvaughn (the God of Reason. Dwells in the West.)

4. Jokahn (is the female emanation of Luvaughn.)

5. Procadius (the God of Industry. Dwells in the East.)

6. Avia (She is the female emanation of Procadius.)

7. Smartallian (the God of Rhetoric. Dwells in the South.)

Love Battles Reason

And one time
Happened three times
And became one time
And gave way
To a form named, Reighlon
The God of love.
He dwells in crystal caverns
That lay in winter's north.
There is no inductive reason
Living within Reighlon.
Once love enters into
The infinite chambers
Of his heart
It clings to the Immortal soul,
Sucking the wind
From all fibers,
Stretching its un-calibrated arms
Across the green glistened dew
Of morning's new birth.
Its milky white winters
Provide shelter from the wrath
Of its blue frozen chasm.
Love knows his passion
Shines like the harvest moon
And burns his sun

Into pleasurable submission.
His ability to induce
Predicated Propositional Thought
Is trapped in love's
Living Intelligible Form.
His inductive observation
Is cloaked in love's eternal womb.
Reighlon spilt his being
To form a bride.
He named her Shaylah.
Her beauty glistens
Like God's illuminating lineament.
Her hair falls like
An eternal waterfall.
Her neck is dressed
In heavenly stars
That permeate her perfect breast.
Her skin flows
Like milk and honey
Across her thighs
And down her knees
Covering her footprints
With love's endless journey.
Her immortal soul
Trappe's the material dimension
In love's physical from.
Her intellect is divided
Into emotional love
While living beings
Negate the contemplation
Of the form of being.

Luvaughn appears on clouds
Of deductive thoughts.
He resides between the furnaces
That burn blood
In the sundrenched Western skies.
He responds with thunder
That echoes through black time
His face covered in ego
As he writes his notes
Into the chronicles of fire.
He notices her luscious lips
As she speaks ba kay sha kosh,
The love language
Of all Immortal Gods.
Luvaughn's mind begins to shatter
Into yellow stained glass.
Shaylah flies in ruby slippers
And fixes her golden gown.
She rolls through clouds of cotton.
Luvaughn is blinded
By her eyes made of jewels
Which see deep within
His cast iron soul.
His pen of steel
Writes out bloody words
That reflect from the constellations.
Shaylah's envious beauty
Causes him to give way
To his mortal needs.
His Lamenting heart
Begins to yearn incessantly.

His infinite jealously
Creates a holy storm
That rages with vengeance.
It begins to measure reason
With an infinite tuning fork.
Its celestial sound
Is separated by an eternal octave,
And through its glorious lens
Luvaughn sees backwards
Into the consciousness
Of Shaylah's overwhelming power.
Luvaughn splits his form
In order to shield himself
From Shaylah's relentless perfection.
His deductive power
Is pulled from his intellect.
His propositional thinking
Is scattered across
The northern lights.
His emanation gives birth to Jokahn,
A female form.
She arrives in winter's chariot
To suck the colors from fall.
Shaylah uses paper chains
To hold her captive.
The battle of jealousy
Takes place on a field
Of black day.
Jokahn divides herself
Into seven legions
That divide themselves

Into twelve war horses.
Their nostrils rain chaos
Their eyes cross space and time.
While Shaylah's cannons
Echo through eternity
Jokahn forms a battle line
Across a field of razors
And love's murderous soul
Spreads like an aspen forest
And swallows up death.
Jokahn begins to wither
Like poison berries
On winter's forgotten vine.
Luvaughn appears in a place
Where time doesn't exist.
He fills his pen of deceit
With the blood
From all mortal forms
Who seek to destroy
Love's unconditional wrath.
For he who is remembered
Will be forgotten
And he who is forgotten
Will be remembered
And love's hermaphrodite form
Is fortified by the One.
The iron pen of reason
Engraves its blood red words
Upon a war-thirsty tongue.
It shaves the skin
Of the subconscious mind

Down to imprisoned bones.
Luvaughn slowly molts
His wings of fire
Upon the self-righteous forms
Serving up Libations
Of intoxicating knowledge.
Wisdom hides its eternal clock
As it reposes in moral virtue.
Luvaughn ciphers divine knowledge
Through his pierced heart.
His senses are caught
In summer's envious heat.
Truth is falling freely
In love's eternal abyss.
Luvaughn's subconscious awareness
Cries out to inductive reasoning.
But the papacy
Cuts off his tongue
And conciliarism is abolished
While love's eternal form
Is welded into the intellect
Of living beings
That pose both
Deductive and inductive reasoning.

End of Book 1

The Book of Rhetoric

Smartallian licks his brain
While it cages
His angry thoughts.
His southern hospitality
Rains blood on all spectre.
His tongue spits out fire
Of proportional discourse,
Words that skew
The reality of his constituency.
Smartallian drowns the logic
Of mortal men
That prosper on jealous ego,
Their envious desire
Lamenting in corroded flesh.
The mortals cling to Smartallian's
Self-righteous vindication.
Smartallian sits on the edge of time
And preaches in deductive language
As he blindfolds reality.
He beats the anvil of ambiguity
That echoes through the intellect
Of all forms of being.
He substantiates false conclusions.
He turns truth into death
By removing inductive reasoning

From all who digest
The bile that flows
From his crooked mouth.
He chains propositional thinking
With words that murder
The world's soul
And rapes the consciousness
Of inductive reasoning
From the intellect
Of the forms of being.
Reighlon opens his Golden branches.
His leaves float
On eternity's ever-changing wheel.
His tears fall like dripping blood.
His roots swallow
The patience of eternity
And choking Smartallian's hunger
Shaylah appears to Smartallian
In form's beautiful luster,
Her form so radiant
That it causes his spectre
To fold into the abyss.
His soul spreads
Across the blue north wind,
Swallowing up silver clouds.
Lightning bolts are born
From Shaylah's yellow eyes.
Her skin is dressed
In brown milky silk.
Her breasts are covered
In colors of fall.

Her thighs spread
Across love's eternal canvas.
Smartallian stretches his mind
And starts to bend time.
His lust for Shaylah
Starts to rain deception
Over his grey dominion.
Luvaughn's conceited veins
Are filled with black pride
As he cast down
His incessant storm of confusion.
His pen of solid steel
Erases all rationale.
His emotions are blinded
By words that Peirce
The eyes of his soul.
His rage descends
On the fire
Of hell's naked chest.
He divides all mortal consciousness
Into nine days.
His thoughts spread
Like ravaging tree roots
Swallowing up the earth's crust.
His incessant furnace burns
With envious fires
From the sun of Venus.
He uses it to melt
Iron from Earth's eternity.
His ladle scoops up
The Milky Way.

He pours his thoughts
Around the limbs
Of all mortal beings.
But when he poured
His envious reason
Around the Skelton of Smartallian
It turned his days to black
And his nights into oblivion.
Smartallian's anger enslaves
The spectre of Luvaughn.
He hammers corroded nails
Into the material dimension
Of all captive souls.
He rips apart Earth's orbit
And throws it into
Eternity's endless treadmill.
Four ages pass through
The dismal abyss.
Smartallian pours iron lava
Into the mouth
Of all mortal men.
He shoots arrows of pain
From his diamond chariot.
His space black war horses
Gallop through bones
Of eternal clocks.
Reighlon swims his way
Through thick lavender clouds
Of dialectical chaos.
His tears fall
Like bloody boulders

Across the faces
Of all human forms.
He drinks the abstract thesis
That pours through the minds
Of all who are subjugated
By Smartallian's skewed reality.
Reighlon begins to pull time
Through a lamenting vortex
That is held together
With frozen Rhetoric.
Reighlon throws down
His gentle scepter
And stretches his arms
Across the eternal abyss.
He reaches down
To the deepest black hole
And cuts it into four corners.
The sons of men
And every soul terrified
As Reighlon drinks
The red fires of hell.
Smartallian takes a blind refuge
On moon's lamenting gravity
While Reighlon pours
His love in the oceans of grace.
Now Luvaughn opens
His book of iron
And calls upon Jokahn
To read his words of blood.
Her cries resonate
Through the black void

As they propagate
Across the constellations.
Smartallian's rage is captured
In gates of fire.
He tells Jokahn
To pierce the tongues
Of all mortal humanity.
His fiery antithesis
Is extinguished by Jokahn's
Voice of jagged acuity.
Smartallian rises up
From the red ashes
And splits his form
Into ages of ignorance
That consume all senses
Of the forms of being.
He severs the thoughts
Of truth and justice.
He summons the eternal plow
But the fields are bleeding.
Lo, the mortal spirits
That smile through blind hypocrisy.
Reighlon folds up
The four corners of space and time.
He rips apart the limbs
Of egotistical ignorance.
He pours their souls
Upon clouds of fire.
Shaylah appears in a gown of gold;
Her beauty illuminates the heavens.
Luvaughn raises his glass pen

And dips it into
Love's eternal promise
As Jokahn ratifies
God's ultimate synthesis.

End of Book 2

The Industrial Reckoning

And two times happened five times.
Procadius beats his brass ribcage
With diamond knives.
His eastern cold winds
Sharpen his poison thistles,
Impregnating the souls
Of the impure dimension
With a craving
For material lust.
His eyes emerald green
Peirce through heaven's eternity.
His perfect teeth
Shine like white ivory.
His capitalistic abyss
Is filled with hollow prayers
From the souls
Of mortal forms.
Now Procadius brings forth
His Golden harp.
He plucks the eighth
And ninth string.
His harmonious sound
Penetrates the fibers
Of all humanity
And one by two

And four by six
Procadius begins to suck
The air that fills
The infinite lungs
Of mortal beings.
He makes love
To the blood red sun
That burns from his furnaces.
He melts the skin
From the mortals
That concur with his
Lustful industry.
He then folds
Red Rock Mountains
Into the dying sea.
He carves an eternal path
Through crumbling mountains.
He forces the sun to set
Into life's eternal labor.
He drags the moon
Across the stars
As he feeds
The Golden lion
While it rips apart
The limbs of all humanity.
Smartallian rises up
Through lamenting clouds
Of poison rain.
While Procadius manufactures
Bloody words of Rhetoric
He snatches the thoughts

Off of Smartallian's brain
Before they reach his tongue.
He uses man-made religion
To boggle the minds
Of human intellect.
He bifurcated the words
Of Smartallian's speech.
He uses the hammers
Of the Demiurge
To forge the thoughts
Of hatred in his subordinates.
He summons the magical tongues
Of prideful clergyman
Who seek to destroy
The earth and all its wonders.
In the name of God
Porcadious chains the thoughts
Of Smartallian's bliss.
He forms crooked words
Through non-discursive reasoning.
Purple waves of ignorance
Fill the void
Of rational thinking.
Truth is divided
By eternity's false pride.
Human thoughts commute
On rivers of blood.
Procadius incarcerates religion
With Smartallian's iron lips.
He creates a vision
Of the almighty God

In the form
Of a blind mirror,
A God that has
Never declared war
Upon the souls
That dwell within
The material dimension.
Procadius assembles an illusion
That convinces humanity
That their demiurge
Possess the capacity
For moral thought.
Luvaughn appears in blood-stained boots.
He takes on a laborer's form.
His stomach turns inside out.
His hands are callused
By the tongs of fire.
His lips are chapped
By the northern compass.
Fire starts to rain down.
Luvaughn starts to talk to himself
First in English, and then in Spanish,
Then French, and now Portuguese.
His soul is ripped
And spread across
The four corners of hell.
He labors in vain
As Procadius beats him
With an iron belt.
Drenched in fire
Procadius raises his voice

And it echoes through the void.
Boasting and laughing
He begins his monstrous articulations
And starts his industrious wrath.
He says, "I have given you vipers for priests.
I have given you
Dogs for teachers.
I have forced worms to beg
For the dirt they eat.
I sold the thief
The right to suck the bones
Of innocent men.
I've taken the sun
And caused it to burn
The life out of all mortal men.
I have raped the moon
Of it illuminating lineament.
What is the price for freedom?
Is it death?
No! You have given me
Your dwelling, your wife and your children."
Luvaughn divides himself
Into two separate forms:
One male, and one female.
They divide themselves
Into an infinite army of one.
Procadius yields the harvest
Of labor's bloody bounty.
He rides his eternal war chariot
Into finite existence.
Luvaughn cries out

Through the earth's crust.
He drives death's plow
Over the callused bones
Of industrious nations.
He measures the time of fools
With an infinite clock
While wisdom goes untouched.
He lights an eternal inferno
That melts liquid prosperity
Into words of ambiguous law.
He binds the minds
Of wounded souls
With gullible reasoning
While Procadius sows doubt
Into the flesh of existence.
He portrays knowledge
As the face of Satan.
He has the questions
But never the answers.
He renders fear and pestilence
And addresses it as wisdom.
He laughs, while labor's soul
Ties itself to a Lamenting wheel
That turns into non-entity.
Procadius gives birth
To the emanation, Avia.
She gives birth
To the sons of war
And her daughters
Give birth to death.
Procadius orders all humanity

To murder their own soul
With labor, love, war and pestilence.
He rides high
On his diamond war chariots.
Reighlon rises up
Through bloody ashes
Wielding his righteous sickle.
His trumpets call out
To the souls
Of all Immortal forms.
He summons the moon
To bring light
Into the dark abyss.
He reaches into the skulls
Of the eternal world.
He gives vision to the wind
As he pokes out the eyes
Of the human mind.
Luvaughn opens up
The ocean of eternity
And exposes the bones of war.
Procadius descends through bronze clouds
Proclaiming he is God of all gods.
Shaylah appears in crystal form.
Procadius rotates to the South
And turns love into war.
He gathers his Golden war horses
And divides himself into calloused pride
While Shaylah and Reighlon
Feast on the world's flesh
And drink the earth's blood.

The mountains flee
Into a mundane state
Of green consciousness.
Eternal reality is distorted.
Trees are born without bark.
Flowers bloom without color.
The wind blows motionless.
Thunder is silenced
Through the center
Of gentle hurricanes.
Procadius descends from
Black morning's fog.
He turns truth
Into dead roses.
He splits heaven's gates
Into winter's rage.
He beats on steel
Drums of war.
He calls on Mars
To rain blood
On the stars of Shaylah.
Procadius casts eternal chains
Around the western plow
As he chops the sun
Into four pieces
And lays them across
The northern sphere.
Reighlon ascends from
The Rolling veins of hell
His Imagination conceives a form
That is translucent in color.

He opens himself up
And extracts the nucleus
From time and space.
He injects Jokahn's soft reasoning
Into the jagged hearts
And mechanical brains
Of all forward marching mortals.
While Shaylah plants
The infinite seeds
Of the almighty God
Into the material soul
Of Procadius's spectre
Avia appears on
Spiraling clouds of reckoning.
She walks on raindrops
As her skin of silk
Covers the eyes
Of Luvaughn's divine mind.
Her curves rain temptation.
Her womb is howling.
Shaylah circles eternity
In her clad of iron.
Procadius brings forth
His majestic artillery.
Bloody cannonballs fall
From his loins
Into the groaning soul
Of Shaylah's spectra.
Her Immortal soul
Is captured by
The mid dimension.

Reighlon finds her
And quenches her thirst
With heavens rain
That pours from
An inverted cloud
That rides the northern stars.
He embalms her soul
And sows it
Into his heart.
Reighlon turns to Procadius
And divides him into twelve
And tethers him
To the horns
Of hell's dragon.
He is commissioned
By the One
To drink hell's eternal fire
Until all mortal forms
Are reimbursed tenfold.

The Saving of Immortal Souls

Reighlon splits his intellect
And plants the Form of Being
Into the veins
Of all mortal beings.
He injects Divine Motion
Into all individual intellect
As he shackles
The tongue of Smartallian.
He turns inside out
And sees his immortal soul.
He splits his form of being
Into seven continents.
He contemplates nature
And forms an imitative
Vortex that shapes reality.
His hypostasis soul
Illuminates fallen shadows
While he hammers nails
Into the world's soul.
Skewed reality flows
Through the crosscut fingers
Of Smartallian's endless roots.
Reighlon tries to paste
Devine Propositional thinking
Back into the individual intellect.

However, brains are branded
With non-discursive rhetoric.
Reighlon immediately cuts
The soul from the sun
And covers up
The World's soul
With burning rays of truth.
He takes the form of intellect
And tosses it
Across the universe.
He swallows individual intellect
And it courses through
His digestive system.
He then welds the parts
Of the individual intellect
Into the Whole Intellect.
He plants the seeds
Of all individual souls
Back into the hypostasis soul.
He cremates the mind of Lavuaghn
And spreads the ashes
Across an infinite milky way.
He makes eternal love
To Shaylah's human form
And she gives birth
To a new level of consciousness.
Luvaughn's soul is reincarnated.
He rises above
The realm of discursive reasoning
And providential order
Takes its place.

Inside the World's soul
A simple revolution
Starts to permeate
Within the sensible world.
Eternity turns into a single day.
Infinity is molded into a single night.
Reighlon slowly weaves
The bodies of
The material World
Into the lowest power
Of the World's Soul.
He swallows the world's soul
And spits it out
Across the sublunary sphere.
He calls upon Shaylah
To activate the soul
Of the sun.
Shaylah begins to council
The soul of the stars
And the moon.
Heaven begins to realign itself
With the workings
Of the World's Soul.
Now the Earth God
Redeems the soul
Of all bleeding plants.
Now Reighlon calls
Upon the Earth's divine soul
To eradicate the sense perception
Of all divine souls
That are in concert

With God's providential order.
Reighlon rolls his eyes
To the back of his brain.
He severs the bodies
That dwell in the souls
Of the material dimension
Into two separate parts
And calls them
The higher soul
And the lower soul.
He commands the lower soul
To exercise discursive thinking
Within the Sensible World.
He authorizes the higher soul
To be cognizant
In the Intelligible World.
He then shreds
The Confusion that lives
In distorted human souls
By filtering human bodies
Through divine purification.
He then restores
Human souls to the intelligible world.
He stiches power
Into the lower soul.
He dresses the lower soul
In eternal sense perception.
The lower soul
Gives birth to
The faculty of presentation.
Mortal bodies become empowered

With the powers
Of the soul.
He then reaches
Out to Shaylah.
They lay together
In a field of
Soft cotton clouds.
They make infinite love
And Shaylah gives birth
To sensory affection.
The earth starts
To spin backwards
Through a red abyss.
Sense perception yields
Its power of presentation
To sensory affection
Which yields its power
To the soul of nature.
Reighlon qualifies mortal bodies
And cultivates traces of the soul
Which emanate new brains
And new hearts
And new livers.
He begins to heat
His eternal furnace.
He uses the rods of Porcadious
To weld nerves of reason
Into the inverted brains
Of all living beings.
He galvanizes arteries
Into the hearts

Of mortal bodies.
He weaves veins
Into the liver
Of all that breath
He calls upon nature
To cast traces of the soul
Into the new qualified bodies.

The End

Lavaughn's Symphony Philosophical Reckoning

Turn yourself inside out
And without a doubt
Look inside of you.
There are those
That are few,
Only the ones that pursue
Truth in the dark.

No more spiritual hope
In following a preacher.
What's your moral mission
In following a politician?

Turn off your ears
And drink up all your fears,
Let your conscious be clear,
Wipe your eyes of the tears.
Excuses are lame,
Got your own self to blame
For being a pawn in the game.
Got no time for the shame.

So bare the pain
Of a long hard rain.

Fold up the sea
And come back to me.
So what do you say?
Come back today
Untwist the tongues
Of Revolutionary bums.

Piety scrambles
Up your words
Like the songs of song birds.
The truth's gone insane.
Folks will look
Long and hard for you
But won't see a trace
As you stand in their face.

Procadius's Symphony Death Drives The Carriage

Ears fall deaf to the call to beckon
The horse and driver are always second.
To a blood drenched rose killed by marriage
As I reach for hope death drives the carriage.

Wet city streets scream out my name
My flesh is pale, I don't feel the same.
My soul drinks the wine of the raging ferriage
I gasp for breath as death drives the carriage

Have I taken for granted all I've been given?
I start to wonder why I've been living.
My color is gone, my body is harrage
I brace myself as death drives the carriage.

I sacrifice my soul, the earth chews my bones
I weep for the living as they start to moan.
My seed is sown as evidence of my parage
I live forever as death drives the carriage.

Avia's Symphony Does the Executioner Care

The long and celestial walk
To the iron gallows
Intensifies the life blood
That courses through
My rolling veins.
I put one foot
In front of the other
As if I were walking
On an infinite abyss.

My brain is scorched
By the ever approaching
Immortal eternity that inches
Ever so close to the pit of my soul.
My lips quiver in silent fright
As my hands clasp
Onto the thundering chains
Of life's last call.

My legs ache
As they step upon
The crimson gallows of death.
I take my time
For I soon will be knocking
On heaven's infinite door.

But I am at ease;
My consciousness has been taken over
By my subconscious reality,
For I know that death
Is only the beginning.

The priest recites
A hollow prayer
For he thinks God justifies
His blood thirsty ways.
His words fall on deaf ears
Sending his calloused heart
Into chaotic valuations.
The bishop of sympathy
Cries purple tears of sorrow.
The ecumenical body
Slips the anvil noose
Over my sun-drenched neck.
They rejoice in their self-righteousness
For they think God really cares.

The hanger grips the lever.
Cold Sweat rolls
Down her face
Like a black avalanche
That swallows her mind.
She ever so slightly
Starts to pull death's handle
Towards her hollow bosom.
Her blank stare
Forms the conclusion

Of her empty solitude.
She then notices my pain
And jerks the life
From my earthly vessel.

Reighlon's Prayer

Is the crimson leaf
That dies in orange autumn
Born again
On the same branch
In which it dwelled from
In summer's yellow heat?

Does eternal nature die
In the bosom of white winter
Only to be reborn
In the gentle arms
Of Earth's green spring?

Does nature's ego trap me
To the material earth
Even though my Soul
Prepares my thoughts
Of subconscious awareness
As I engage
With my higher self?

My immortal song
Sings eternally
In the material dimension
But resides between the spheres

Of the world's soul
And my divine mind.

As I walk the backwards path
Of solitary enlightenment
I will not be tied
To the material any longer.
Only the immaterial
Pure positive dimension
Can capture my Immortal soul.

Reighlon's Symphony The Almighty Domain

And so it shall be.
God will marry
It's beautiful nature;
For in the beauty of nature
Lies the utmost attribute
Of God almighty's work.

As nature exists in the seasons
God provides the substance
Of nature's discourse.
The almighty erases the notion
Of all freewill
Including the freewill
Within God itself.

The almighty spontaneously reveals
Himself in substance
That exists within
The totality of the infinite.
God's attributes are created
In the modes
Of human existence.

God cuts the piety
Of anthropomorphic religion

By presenting the almighty power
Through the wrath of nature.
Who dares to ride the thunder
While chasing lightning bolts
Over the clouds of God's domain.